Inheritance
with a High Error Rate

INHERITANCE WITH A HIGH ERROR RATE

POEMS

JEN KARETNICK

Cider Press Review

San Diego

INHERITANCE WITH A HIGH ERROR RATE

Cider Press Review
PO BOX 33384
San Diego, CA, USA
ciderpressreview.com

First edition
10 9 8 7 6 5 4 3 2 1 0

ISBN: 9781930781641
Library of Congress Control Number: 2023938636
Cover Illustration "Whale Shark" © Helen Ahpornsiri
    Licensed by Jehane Ltd
Author photograph by Zoe Cross
Book design by Caron Andregg

Winner of the 2022 *Cider Press Review* Book Award:
CIDERPRESSREVIEW.COM/BOOKAWARD.

Printed in the United States of America
at Bookmobile in Minneapolis, MN USA.

For Jon,
always my beloved,
and for Mango House,
always in my heart

Acknowledgements

My heartfelt appreciation goes to a number of people, without whom this book wouldn't exist. I wish bushels of sun-kissed mangoes and hand-gathered peacock feathers to:

My namaste/namaslay girls Catherine Esposito Prescott and Caridad Moro-Gronlier, for having my back and encouraging me to keep going even when the signs seem to point in the opposite direction.

My *SWWIM* and Miami PoetAs Collective sisters Mary Block, Alexandra Lytton Regalado, Emma Trelles, Mia Leonin, Elisa Albo, and Rita Maria Martinez, for your unwavering friendship.

Sandy Yannone, whose perfect advice and assistance came at just the right time. IYKYK.

The talented poet and judge Lauren Camp, who chose this book out of so many other possibilities.

Caron Andregg, Catherine Friesen, Beth McDermott, and the entire editorial staff at *Cider Press Review,* who make such lovely books and journals.

My parents, who have supported me with everything from my first typewriter to my first computer, and my mother-in-law, who faithfully attends all my Zoom readings (and brags about them, too).

My sister, Betsy, the best-y sister who is also my best-y friend, and all my siblings-in-law, for your support over the decades.

My children, Zoe and Remy, and my husband, Jon, for their tolerance of my "hoarding" habits and strange poetic obsessions. Your love keeps me whole. I hope mine keeps you.

Artists in Residence in the Everglades for a stunning month-long stay in Everglades National Park, where several of these poems were composed and many others envisioned.

Deborah Briggs and The Betsy Hotel, for a munificent residency in the legendary Writer's Room, where some of these poems were written and others were inspired.

The Maryland Transit Administrations' Purple Line Writers' Program, whose big-hearted grant while I was teaching full-time allowed me the grace to create many of these pieces.

The Vermont Studio Center, whose all-too-generous fellowship and residency allowed me the space and time to make the final version of this manuscript.

The editors of *Gold Wake Press, Jacar Press,* and *The Word Works,* who named this manuscript a finalist/semi-finalist in their competitions (under a different title), giving me faith to continue on the journey.

The editors and judges of the following journals, anthologies, podcasts, and competitions, who found value in the individual poems here (some published under different titles):

About Place, "I embrace myself as a long-hauler," "Spraying for Zika: A Lesson in the Hydrology Cycle in the Everglades"
Alyss, "Promise City by the Numbers"
AS, "Antonomasia"
The Bangor Literary Review, "I praise my neighbors"
Blue Lyra Review, "Miami: 10 Things You Don't Know About Me"
Cigar City Poetry Journal, "Bodies of Evidence"
Crab Orchard Review, "Slough Slogging in the Dry Season"
The Dodge, "Searching for the Florida Panther, I Find Only Signs"
The Fourth River, "Play, with Foreign Object," "The Nature of Nurture"
The Indianapolis Review, "Self Help Q-and-A at Zoo da Maia"
Limp Wrist, "Evaporating Villanelle for Algae Bloom"
Michigan Quarterly Review, "I Commiserate with the Pygmy Octopus Found in the Miami Beach Parking Garage"
Mom Egg Review Vox Online Quarterly, "After We Move, We Learn about the Miami Supreme: A Matriarchal Shrub," "Babka"
Negative Capability, "On the Compound"
The Odet, "At Riverbend Park"
One, "Face Value"
Painted Bride Quarterly, "The Physics of Falling Mangoes"
Passager Journal, "Flight Plan"
Pilgrimage Press, "The Fragrance Wheel (Part II)"
Poetica Magazine, "I Sit Shiva for the Village That Raised Me"
South Florida Poetry Journal, "I regret eating freedom for breakfast"
The Spectacle, "In the Photic Zone"
Sweet: Lit, "It's about the dog, but not really about the dog,"

Temenos, "Green Iguana Freeze"

Terra Preta Review, "A Contrapuntal of Light-Dependent Reactions"

Terrain, "Mango: An Inheritance with a High Error Rate"

Tinderbox Poetry Journal, "The Foundation of the Number Six (Is Family and a Harmonious Home)"

Under a Warm Green Linden, "Evaporating Villanelle for Emotion #2," "I Live at Ground Zero of the Climate Exodus; Or, How to Sell a Waterfront Home in Miami"

Valparaiso Poetry Review, "The Fragrance Wheel (Part I)," "Trophic Cascade," "The Sound of Zero Copula"

Waxwing, "Rooster Blues"

The Westchester Review, "My Hairstylist Is a Man Who Loves the Shape of a Woman's"

Whale Road Review, "Soccer Mom Weather," "Yard Work"

The Worcester Review, "I Pose / For a Selfie with Venom / My Termite Service Technician / Who Is Still Sometimes Recognized as His Nineties UFC Persona,"

"I Commiserate with the Pygmy Octopus Found in the Miami Beach Parking Garage" is included in the anthology *Octopus* (ed. Lana Hechtman Ayers, World Enough Writers, 2023).

"Searching for the Florida Panther, I Find Only Signs" and "Slough Slogging in the Dry Season" are included in the anthology *Campfire Stories Vol. II* (eds. Ilyssa Kyu and Dave Kyu, Spring 2023, Mountaineer Books)

"Elegy for a Gambler" is included in the anthology *The Book of Life After Death* (ed. Tim Lindner, Tolsun Books, 2023).

"Evaporating Villanelle for Emotion #2" and "I embrace myself as a long-hauler," are collected in *Essential Voices: A COVID-19 Anthology* (eds. Alvarez, Gemme, Hill, and Ivy, West Virginia University Press, 2023).

"Birkat HaBayit: A Woman Is a Bird When" won the 2020 *Tiferet* Writing Contest for Poetry.

"Play, with Foreign Object" was selected for *Poetic License,* a collaborative project between the Poetry Barn and the Arts Society of Kingston, and exhibited with the artist's interpretation in August 2020.

"The Foundation of the Number Six (Is Family and a Harmonious Home)" was a finalist in the 2019 *Tinderbox Poetry Journal* Poetry Contest.

"Face Value" is included in the anthology *Show Us Your Papers* (Main Street Rag, 2020).

"I regret eating freedom for breakfast" is included in the anthology *Is It Hot in Here or is it Just Me? Women Over Forty Write on Aging* (Beautiful Cadaver Project Pittsburgh, 2019).

"Considering Chagrin" is included in the anthology *Waters Deep: A Great Lakes Poetry Anthology* (Split Rock Review Press, 2018).

"There's Banishment for Native Eyes in Sight of Native Air" is included in the anthology *AFTERMATH* (Radix Media, 2018).

"It's about the dog, but not really about the dog," was nominated for a 2019 Best of the Net Award.

"Flight Plan" won an honorable mention in the 2019 *Passager Journal* Poetry Contest and in the 2019 Stephen A. DiBiase Poetry Contest. It also appears in the anthology *Rewilding: Poems for the Environment* (Flexible Press, 2020).

"Elegy for a Gambler" was a finalist in the 44th New Millennium Awards for Poetry and was published in *New Millennium Writings.*

"The Physics of Falling Mangoes" was featured on the *PDQ Slushpile* podcast, episode 10, on June 15, 2016.

"At Riverbend Park" won the 2016 Romeo Lemay competition from *The Odet* magazine.

Part II of "The Fragrance Wheel" appeared in the Sweat Broadsheet exhibit, accompanying artist Raul Perdomo's painting, and was featured at the Miami Book Fair International 2014.

"Green Iguana Freeze" was first published in the chapbook *Landscaping for Wildlife* (Big Wonderful Press, 2013).

Contents

I.

"One evening
I met the mango."

—Mary Oliver

I Commiserate with the Pygmy Octopus Found in the Miami Beach Parking Garage

First time? I get it. In this place, it's inevitable
to cling to cement like forgotten spaghetti
in the bottom of the pot. Bottom dwellers, holders

of the smallest hopes, we have so much in common.
Always it's a rude awakening to find yourself flush
on the floor under the neon glare of a super beaver

moon, the surging sea a near distance, that uterine shed
of toxic algae, the sick-room stink sweeping in long
before the scarlet-feathered dawn, pushing you into

a place you never thought you'd go. All three of your
hearts were born to know what dying is, but this is
different: only air beats through your gills to replace

their copper charges. *Canary in the coalmine of climate
change,* marine biologists call you. *Expect more sea
creatures in dry spaces.* Twitter sends recipes, sarcasm.

*This is from the city that brought the world a shark
on the Metrorail. Is it running for mayor?* Harbinger
or hoax, but alive when security scoops you into a bucket

of saltwater and deposits you home—the question is not
how long can you survive out of the ocean, but why should
we have to see your blood to know how much bluer it runs?

The Physics of Falling Mangoes

If a Haden mango, full with sun,
and an ovoid Irwin, that ornament
of dawn, drop at the same time from
panicles equivalent in height,
will they accelerate identically
despite degrees of heft, of maturity,

the knowledge of their own ripeness?
Physics says yes, no matter mass, even
if it's a late-season Beverly, still green,
set upon too early by a squirrel
sitting on its stem, or an Indian mango
five pounds large, swaying all summer,

too big for the basket of the tool
I wield like lightning to strike
a singular fruit. The damage, then:
that should be equal, too. But all things
considered, there is no free fall. Air,
on a humid whim, can change

its resistance, and there is no formula
to adjust for the destructive means
of a mango during descent, helicoptering
sap through the day's work of spider webs,
a season of boat-shaped leaves that bear
those burns until they themselves release,

and the twigs it breaks without discrimination,
whether they are ready to reach like hands
or be struck down to ground. And the ground,

which could be oolite or limestone, grass
or a brother mango, the driveway
or the chemical buffer of pool water,

my shoulder or arm or skull, willing to take
the aromatic knock. I know the parts
of the equation: limb, fruit, gravity. But not
the sum, upon landing. Wholly bruised? Flesh
protected by deflection? Or a split that, turned
every possible way, simply grants a smile?

Evaporating Villanelle for Algae Bloom

We all have secrets we would like to keep
to ourselves. Sure, the sea is no different.
The whole grave mass of it could cover up

oil spills, plastics. But they spike into shape,
those hourglass whorls to see in the distance.
We all have secrets we would like to keep

but still resuscitate. Regret's lewd,
a sour bite that shows up for tea;
the whole grave mass of it could

foul the interstitial brood
with its vast swirl, its Milky Way.
We all have secrets we would

label scarlet tide or sea snot—
endless whirl of dishonor—
the whole grave mass of it

we fail to save
with mere skimmers,
this whole grave
we all have.

The Gee Whiz Element of
Tropical Storms and Symphonies

During the opening of the hurricane,
the water drains, a rapid decrescendo,

from the shoreline. As silent as sand,
we gather dinner, our nets replete with

those flounder neaped before the coming
movement, caught on a shard of harbor

as if on the ego of a king. We explore
with a microburst of confidence gusting

as hard as the earth's last heated, swollen
breaths. But this lazy adagio will not hold,

written to return like a horn section da capo,
da capo. If we're lucky, we will escape

before the *pour accelerato,* before the thunder
so tympanic we're held captive and captivated,

spectator and spectered, carried away on
a diaphragmatic surge to a horizon that we can't

see and are able, despite such fine-tuned
percussion, to deny how this ending could be so.

Green Iguana Freeze

With a fragment of Sappho

"Sweetbitter unmanageable
creature who steals" into my pool,

eats his share of fruit and then some,
he dives into this stolen freedom

from live oak or deck rail,
unripe to the tip of his tail.

Non-native, also not welcome,
he dives into this stolen freedom

offered by lackadaisical
predators, where plenty can fill

his prehistoric, hollow drum.
He dives into this stolen freedom

then he leaves it behind foul
with his fibrous mango stool

and chews a hole through the mesh frame.
He dives into this stolen freedom

while the weather lasts, while
the pythons in the swamp still rule,

testing my love of the kingdom.
He dives into this stolen freedom,

but when the wind turns to a chill
that portends cold-blooded hell,

I'll fan the flames to keep warm
his stiff-legged dive to freedom.

Slough Slogging in the Dry Season

We plant our poles in Pa-hay-okee peat
—some like fragile seeds we wish to see grow,
some as if to reach the layer of oo-
lite—and follow with dense, tentative feet
dressed in the skins of animals we hope
to avoid in the sheet flow where we are
not the enabled apex predator.
Sun-swaddled, we grapple with poise, grope
the air for miniature enemies,
wade toward the shadows of the cypress dome,
where the panther makes her diurnal home
and alligators stake their territories.
There we post selfies to prove bravery,
leave behind the whiff of chicanery.

The Nature of Nurture

At dusk, the screech owls warn us with a bounce
of song that we've come too near the recesses
they've accessed, their found nests, in the live oaks.

They target heads—ours, and the dogs we walk.
We wear bright-brimmed hats, neon the collars
of the animals, brighten cell phone

screens to announce our presence. But such small,
otherworldly suns fool just a few. One
night, a fly-by swooping cranes us upward.

We find an owl, melting into her
tiled backsplash of brown, beige, and dun,
guarding a duckling?—yes, a wood duckling,

tiny crest of head beginning to green,
peeking out from behind the bird who warmed
a rogue egg enough to hatch it. But he hears

the slide whistle of his mother along
the canal and jumps from the limb to land
unharmed in the swale we have neglected

to trim. Even the dogs pause as he runs
to his kin. Only the owl now fills the space.
Feathering her hollow. Settling. Settling.

On the Compound

The jam pots simmer on the stove, burping
volcanic splatter when the lids are removed.
This one wafts ginger; that one breathes
chilies; a third puffs vanilla and cinnamon.

We have already stuffed the freezer chest with quarts
of diced fruit for smoothies and sangrias; chopped
the chutneys, pickles, and salsas; loaded the dry
sauna of the dehydrator to run for twelve hours

at a time and turn the odd, slippery bits into strips
of toothsome leather. We are making the best
of a too-early bounty, the trees dumping hundreds
of pieces of fruit daily before school has released

for the summer, before help can be ordered
from the children as if from a menu, although danger
under the branches is as constant as myth
and persistent as rumor. To gather mangoes,

you must protect your head and watch your footing,
guard against the inhaling of bugs that zip
like synapses, burrowing into the craters where
the lava of sap has burned holes. Your arms

burst into blooms of sinew; your thighs squat
until the muscles stand stiff as beaten egg whites.
There is no need for gyms and Pilates programs
during season, when heavy with molten juice

each mango is a barbell, and every bag
is a medicine ball we are determined to haul,
and equally desperate to drop. On the compound,
the fruits of our labor must be transformed before

they rot, before it's for naught, and what we eat and drink
later this year is not the sweetness of victory over the due
course of nature in the subtropics but the preservation
of all that we have given, gladly or not, to this exercise.

In the Photic Zone

When the glaciers have calved
so much of their weight that the matter

of my home changes state, bring me
the whales, those Cuisinarts of the ocean,

flat beating the layers of the sea
like cake batter with each deep

dive and sound, icing the surface
with expulsions of iron-rich

excrement that feeds the drift
of sunlight. What we think we own

will no longer be ours to claim,
but the leaves of every book

we've ever read, libraries
of poems lingering in the water

like sonar, will green
and green and green and green.

Spraying for Zika: A Lesson in
the Hydrology Cycle in the Everglades

Poison falls from the sky.
It is not rain but it is like rain,
sent down in a mist from airplanes
flying as low and determined
as ospreys looking for breakfast.
Poison falls from the sky.
It is not rain but it is in the rain
hitting the shaved wicks
of the gumbo limbo and the wax
of fetterbush and bitterwood,
canoeing down elliptic tips unless
it is drought, when the leaves
will gutter what they need for longer.

Poison falls from the sky.
It is millions of missiles unleashed
when the sun is poking up
like a fresh shoot of turtle grass
or dehydrating the horizon, aimed
at the insects carrying blood
diseases that harm the human
unborn, the not-yet-conceived,
the maybe-one-day, the just-in-case,
though plumage can be worn
to prevent a proboscis stick,
and no venom is dropped
to stop what is purely recreational.

Poison falls from the sky
to kill the food that is eaten
by the fish who will be targeted
by bigger fish and who will become
meals for humans worried about
their unborn, the not-yet-conceived,
the maybe-one-day, the just-in-case,
who continue to have sex
without prophylactic inhibitions,
and this poison rusts the chain,
it puddles, it runs off in the river,
intensifying with the tide,
and collects in the bodies of water,

the borrow holes where gravel
was stolen to build yards and roads
where only tracks of bear,
key deer, and panther once were,
the solution holes formed
by the tannic dissolution of limestone
bedrock, where alligators might find
a vacation home in the dry
winter season, the ponds as dark
as immorality, where the wading
birds snap at whatever touches them
with reflexes faster than any proverbial cat.
Poison falls from the sky

into these bodies of water, which become
the still-pool embodiments
of death, of too many bodies who drink it,
who swim in it, who call it *natural
habitat.* Poison falls from the sky
and is taken back up by the ever-present

heat ironing the hammocks, forming
clouds that every late afternoon grow
too pregnant with their earthly cargo,
and punctuate the blue with a rage
that breaches, that can never be
too loudly or righteously expressed,
but that must always, somehow, be borne.

Aubade for Birds

We are not allowed to write poems about birds
anymore, the poet at the podium said before

she read her piece about pelicans. There were already
too many verses about insectivorous swallows

eating on the wing, barn owls making spirited daylight
appearances and, oh, the amount of murmurations

has made the poor, darling starling a visible cliché.
So I won't bore you with the details except to say

on this one morning I heard the microwave tweet
and the coffeemaker squawk, and it was only until

they had sung for several minutes that I realized
it wasn't my husband's breakfast but the yard of birds,

advising me that the day was now ready to open.

Miami: 10 Things You Don't Know About Me

I leap tall tales in a single bound.
My oceans are a Pachanga, held fermata.
The ghosts who haunt me never take a vacation.
I welcome the invaders of all my bodies.

My oceans are a Pachanga, held fermata.
My winds make no ladylike edits.
I welcome the invaders of all my bodies.
I give you the right to be forgotten.

My winds make no ladylike edits.
My disabilities will also become yours.
I give you the right to be forgotten.
The only language I recognize is my own.

My disabilities will also become yours.
You may find that I am a shifting foundation.
The only language I recognize is my own.
Upheaval takes solid root in me.

You may find that I am a shifting foundation.
I welcome the invaders of my body.
Upheaval takes solid root in me.
I leap tall tales in a single bound.

I Live at Ground Zero of the Climate Exodus;
Or, How to Sell a Waterfront Home in Miami

With every king tide the land loosens a little more
around me, a floral caftan to wear after surgery.

Underground, the concrete walls of the houses spall,
crackling like cellophane. The iguanas seem strong

now, flexing their tails and shitting in pools with typical
arrogance, far more equipped to survive than I am,

but one day they will be cut off from the mainland,
the distances too far to swim, the woolly mammoths

of the millennial generation. Left to inbreed, their genes
will become asteroids of their ancestors' making.

It's too late for the maybe-someday, the if-or-when day.
Even the least honest Realtors acknowledge where not

to buy, if you're local, know which communities are
a harder sell—these they peddle to half-timers who can

afford to have no wind insurance or worry, who private
jet away from storms into the peace of other primary

residences, where peacocks don't stalk the roads, chevroned
by dried saline, attracted to the fish and frogs left behind

when the water recedes like a hairline, leaving its prickly
evidence of once-was. This is how it is to long for something

I haven't even left yet, steeped in nostalgia like old tea
leaves that have barely any hue and even less future to give,

like the beaches here, bony under mounds of the sargassum
smothering the sea turtles, the crabs and lobsters. Oh, the static,

interstitial species. How they, too, can't obey the logic to go
when the draw is so magnetic to stay. Still, I plug the address

of every available house into the FEMA Flood Map Service Center,
bury Saint Joseph upside-down near the "For Sale" sign, pray that

his discomfort in the dark will lead me to some kind of light—
    homes
built on natural oolite ridges or manufactured rises, complete with

impact windows and hurricane-proof doors—and every day watch
the statue's feet get washed by the mother who is all of our toxic

mothers, protrude a little more from the eroding ground, leaning
inland, inland, inland, where we will both be reborn as eventuality.

Mango: An Inheritance with a High Error Rate

The slick gush of you. The stain and stick
of you. How you fill cheeks like the residue
of a tongue bitten nearly in two. The way
you linger in the air with the fleetest of flies
no one can catch except with leftover wine
rotting in wide-mouthed glasses along with
the lead points of bodies I collect like coins

until the liquid chokes with them. This is about
how I've loved you for so long I've grown weary
of you, fragrant wild grenades percussing through
the night onto the shards of the pool deck,
pinging off drainpipes and catching in gutters,
splattering the slats of the solar panels with
such force that I sleep dreaming of ancestral dangers.

And all the abundance you beget, the family members
who clamor for you and bring back breads and chutneys
and salsas made too saccharine with you, dishes to spoil
in the back of the refrigerator. And your pits that root
themselves in oolite and silt from squirrel-gnawed fruit,
thrusting up seedlings when no one is looking, that might
or might not bear if allowed to grow, but will be

considered new varieties if you do, those genes
throwbacks to every Asian, Latin, and Caribbean
tree that contributed to your lineages. And those who will
name you, guess again, rename you. And the food
pantries that won't take you even though you are fresh,
unprocessed, because this is no longer how America
embraces anything: in your colorful, foreign-born skins.

Play, with Foreign Object

The octopus found a coconut,
hollow and halved like a locket,

dropped into its world. A chair
waiting for its occupant, the shell

rocked on the ocean floor, inviting
as tea. The octopus lowered its mantle

into the crisp ochre fruit where the meat
once was, and closed the other section

over its head, sliding each of its arms
in from the cracks, leaving not a single

sucker to be caught by edges. And then
it rolled and bounced, propelled by

the predictable tide. And the whole sea
shuddered with this shred of saturated joy.

II.

"When I began to eat
things happened.
All through the sweetness I heard voices."

—Mary Oliver

Flight Plan

At Bill Baggs Cape Florida State Park, for Jennifer
Hull

Because we couldn't take our eyes off the children,
shaking droplets off like anhinga in the sun-greased air,

because I had lost my daughter once on a Naples beach
that year and, already hanging cloth over the mirror

of my heart, thought *Yes, I will forever now be* that *mother,*
because I had been late but my friend had been later

and the waning afternoon was a hunger we were trying to control,
we spoke to each other as if we were driving, our faces in profile.

Peripheral. We saw only the dangers that lay directly ahead
for the smallest-limbed swimmers among us, who were not

really swimmers yet at all, who were awkward in every medium,
coordinated as windchimes in a hurricane. We didn't notice

the silvering fog of the newly installed mist nets, there to catch
neotropical migrating songbirds at the banding station,

barely visible mesh border walls for tanagers and bananaquit
whose wings couldn't beat them through on the way from

Eastern Canada to the Western Caribbean. Capture, it seems,
is for their own good. Typed, sexed, and blooded, they are afterward

let go to feast on the skins of fruits and insects, storing sugars
and proteins in their strong treble bellies for the next leg

of their journeys. Since that summer, 27,402 passerine have been
counted and chronicled, named and noted, some as numerous as

the more than 4,000 ovenbirds, others as rare as MacGillivray's
    mourning
warbler, of which there has been only one. Now children take field
    trips

with their mothers to learn about the sapsuckers and flycatchers.
They climb the lighthouse steps, closed for repair when our
    daughters

were young enough to want to, when our legs were strong enough
to go with them. We wouldn't know any of this as we scrubbed

their cheeks with aloe. Selfish herd. Flock of two by two. Pink suns,
veering together. Mary Oliver wrote that "a poem should always

have birds in it." Perhaps what she meant is that here, in this place,
there can also be no grounding without joy in it. This is how I now
    see

that day: Each child in our arms. Each bird in its net. The horizon,
    filled
with its own swelling promise, also waiting for some kind of release.

Rooster Blues

The just-hatched chicks were let loose as favors.
Barely dry, they were let loose like favors,
a flavicomous cloud dropped among toddlers.

The birthday boy picked them up and held them.
The party guests picked them up and crushed them.
They forgot about the "pet" in petting farm.

We gathered the chicks in a cowboy hat.
Collected chicks in the well of a straw hat,
and took four of them home to make them fat.

We shouldn't have named them after cousins.
We learned never to name birds after cousins.
Ben didn't make it; the others mashed him.

The three grew an aubade of combs: All roosters.
And took to the stew pot our dream of brooders.

Elegy for a Gambler

If it is true that "the dead have all the glory of the world,"¹ then so too do the missing, the lost, the stolen, the runaways, the mentally absent, the Krissy Houstons and Lamar Odoms found with lungs like water balloons, induced into comas with legal drugs, only one of them lucky enough to survive the race back into a society that will no longer offer garlands of roses because "we live... in feelings, not in figures on a dial."² Yet Amber and Silver alerts buzz our phones like low-flying planes with messages begging us to look, implore us to be witnesses, take note, as if in this particular age we are actually more aware of the world around us rather than less, only glancing up from gadgets to avoid walking through glass and into door jambs or knocking our foreheads against the woodpecker-splintered poles supporting these essential wires.

But the first time the unheard-of happens, no such warnings exist, so when the fifty flamingo chicks were snatched from Hialeah Park Race Track one July to be resold on the exotic pet market, "a very profitable thing to be involved in if you're a thief,"³ no Rose or Rouge or Fuchsia alerts were delivered mobile to our inauthentic eyes and ears. No images of birds adorable with fuzz that stood out as if rubbed against rubber to create static electricity were sent for biometric identification. No *If you see this flamingo, please contact...* And perhaps there won't be a next time for this flock who, like so many citizens of this portmanteau city, *exilios* of Cuba, have planted their genetic code in such uncertain, urban earth,

---

1   From the poem "We live in deeds, not years; in thoughts, not breaths" by Philip James Bailey

2   From the poem "We live in deeds, not years; in thoughts, not breaths" by Philip James Bailey

3   Jorge Pino, Florida Fish and Wildlife Conservation Commission

once considered by the natives a "pretty prairie,"[4] for generations now. When giving birth is the original gamble, keeping offspring from harm is merely a show parlay: whatever one gets, they all get. But the thief—he is the first gambler. And he can take many forms: bird wrangler, horse track regular, poker player, brother.

My brother taught me to gamble with pennies on the floor of the den where cave crickets exercised their moon-landing legs the same year the Meadowlands Racetrack was born, the year of his Bar Mitzvah, the year he quit Judaism, the year my parents brought home the Siberian Husky pup he trained to attack and drag me down the stairs by my ankles as if hauling a live crow through snow drifts. Even though he cheated, always claiming the deal, labeling himself the house, I loved my brother enough back then to let him fleece me of my piggy bank savings the way a farmer sticks his hand under a nesting hen for her eggs: I hardly squawked. Learning to play Blackjack, Texas Hold 'Em, Seven Card Stud—these were my own diversionary tactics. Of course they didn't work in the long term; a wager never does pay off that way. For those of us who give too much, there will always be recipients who want nothing in the end. The shared account, bloated by the drop and release of ridged, deliberate coins, waits. This time, when the alert sounds, it's in code, a terse range of monophonic blues that calls all our bets, and never again allows for a raise.

---

4   Hialeah comes from the Muskogee words haiyakpo (prairie) and hili (pretty)

I Sit Shiva for the Village That Raised Me

For Edward and Evelyn Blau

In the house I knew as well as my own,
house that mirrored our split-level floors,
I learned how to house pain when my neighbor
died young, the cancer housed above his frown

lines also found in the too-bronzed house
of his torso. House of mourning, but still
we played house and card games upstairs well
into the night while other households took pause

of their lives to form the house's minyan.
Later, back in my house, I woke to find him
housed in light at the end of my bed, the same
as when he worshipped at the house of the sun.

Now his widow departs this earthbound house.
Vacant house, I wait still for luster after loss.

I embrace myself as a long-hauler, *

lignum vitae, wood
so dense it doesn't float

I've been reduced to not being able to stand up in the shower

poetic, considering how much
the wood has given to ocean travel

Even reading a book is challenging and exhausting

an escaped ornamental
pruned to maintain a narrower profile

I don't understand what's happening in my body

the leaf is made of more
than one leaf-like part

Every day you wake up and you might have a different symptom

from a distance
like clouds of purple

I've had messages saying this is all in your head

as the non-native is not invasive
at the northernmost range

I understand there are so many unknowns

not so easily warped by humidity

or temperature changes

As a patient, I need acknowledgment

as a generalization, then,
it suffers from a reputation as slow

It has gotten better, but I track that trajectory in weeks, not days

similar to pomegranate seeds
either one is a worthwhile endeavor

Being a survivor is something you must also survive

*This poem is comprised of phrases found from the following two articles:

Ed Yong, "COVID-19 Can Last for Several Months," *The Atlantic,* June 4, 2020,
HTTPS://WWW.THEATLANTIC.COM/HEALTH/ARCHIVE/2020/06/COVID-19-
CORONAVIRUS-LONGTERM-SYMPTOMS-MONTHS/612679/
"'Wood so dense it doesn't float'"By Kenneth Setzer Fairchild Tropical Botanic
Garden, *Miami Herald,* August 19, 2016
HTTPS://WWW.MIAMIHERALD.COM/LIVING/HOME-GARDEN/ARTICLE96640832.HTML

@Death Follows Me on Twitter

From a real, defunct Twitter account

@Death tells me our relationship is complicated, and wants to
simplify things.

@Death tells me about "soul midwives" and "death doulas,"
flashlight-armed ushers to that final throne.

@Death tells me to decide now between a 12-piece jazz band and
Rush's 2112 for my service.

@Death tells me that wearing a Fitbit may help me die better:
10,000 steps toward a daily end.

@Death tells me, on the day Wimbledon begins, the history
behind the sudden-death tiebreak. There used to be a
lingering-death tiebreak, too, but that was put to death.

@Death tells me the florists known for reliability and fair pricing.
@Death does not know the scent of flowers aches my temples,
throbs my veins.

@Death tells me the statistics on selfies: officially five times more
fatal than shark attacks.

@Death tells me jokes, like the one about the man who invented
autocorrect dying. "Restaurant in Peace," @Death says.

@Death tells me, when the U.S. women win their fourth World
Cup, that captains of losing teams were traditionally sacrificed.

@Death wants to know if I will put down my surviving pets when I die.

@Death is feeling ancient Egyptian, but walks like a cop in a donut shop.

@Death wants me to take one last rum safari in Jamaica, drink mamajuana with the locals.

@Death tells me that "dying on holiday does happen." Presumably by selfie.

@Death tells me lines from obituaries, such as "Freeda sledge-hammered every rule of healthy eating to obtain a nice long life."

@Death tells me about direct cremation, how I can be turned into ash without a priest. @Death does not know that I'm Jewish, despite skin etched into graphic anecdotes.

@Death tells me stories, like the one about the golden retriever trained to bring tissues to mourners at a funeral home.

@Death asks if I've seen Michael Jackson around. @Death is not old enough to ask about Elvis.

@Death posts links for alternative hearses. My coffin can be carried by a Harley Davidson sidecar, Volkswagen Campervan, horse-drawn carriage, fire engine, vintage truck, bicycle, or Land Rover capable of an off-road detour.

@Death tells me grief will compound chronic pain, speed up an illness.

@Death tells me to appoint a digital executor to care for my social media estate.

@Death tells me how I can be unburied in a coffin made of willow or bamboo that biodegrades so that my bones will be available to the earth, my reception embraceable as limbs. Death does not know that I live at sea level, where mangroves snarl the sand.

@Death tells me how I do and do not feel, twice per day, sometimes three times.

@Death tells me to be #DeathPositive, but so often the numbers say otherwise.

Yard Work

To mow the lawn—his only chore—he propped open
his bedroom window with his stereo speakers, set the arm

so the vinyl would repeat, and turned the volume
louder than the sputter of gas chewing overgrown New Jersey

grass. When Meatloaf screamed about a "Bat Out of Hell,"
the whole neighborhood knew my brother's allowance

was being withheld or he was about to get the belt. My sister
and I used the clippers to trim the curbed edges even though

we also dusted, vacuumed, cooked, and did the dishes,
complaining about unfair divisions of labor one week

to the "Dark Side of the Moon," the next to "The Grand
Illusion" or "Born to Run." We were never allowed to choose

the tunes. My sister grew up to go to Springsteen concerts
with him; I was the one who would truly run from the Northeast,

first to the daily warmth and minty evening breath of Southern
California, then to Miami, moist mouth of the world, where

grass doesn't grow under the mango trees that throw so much
shade there isn't enough sun for such small blades, and where

my brother never came to visit, preferring the green he grew
in Greenwich and on Wall Street. After he died, his son found

a job in South Florida and came to live with us for a time, learning
the names and provenance of this fruit, how to tell the differences

between a Carrie and a Beverly, between the mango that is not
yet ready to be picked and the one that will be cast out

on the driveway overnight if it is not, and how to eat a freshly
caught Haden over the garbage can or sink to save his suit.

He volunteered to gather them, bringing in armloads like
     firewood,
wandering around the patchy lawn as if it were a bocce court,

one ear tuned to the buried beat of the tropics, the other still turned
inward, an antenna vibrating with the silence his father left behind.

The Fragrance Wheel

1.

A second-story wind
heckled the pines
like an older brother,

rattling the intricate necklaces
of Spanish moss, the pinecone
pendants. Under a strobe

of shade and sun, fickle
needles, a green lynx spider,
predator of earworm moths

and honey bees, shivered
between tree and table,
repairing the veins of its web,

trembling like a hand. Dust
flew over the lake as if born
to velocity. Sandhill cranes,

masked with vermilion,
hooted encouragement.
Only that which lay low

to the ground remained
indifferent: branches discarded
like weathered relationships, fire

ant hills where the drones
protect their queens
with pre-programmed devotion.

II.

At the picnic, the trail of ants
is a loose circumference,
each following the message

of what another had inscribed
before him. Ancient perfumers,
none is born an apprentice

but *le nez,* equipped with essential
abilities to follow, capture and lay down
aromatic applications according to

the First Fragrance created
in their realm, identical
to Egg and Queen. Disorder them.

Steer them off course, toward
your sister's sandwich,
your mother's sun-stale dessert.

Physical disruption will
make no difference.
They may be delayed,

but unlike siblings who have
once picnicked together
and are now grown, scattered,

with no insincere scent
to interpret, ants are anointed,
even after death, by faith.

Babka

*"What they lacked in richness they made up for
'with the delightful swirls,' and the inclusion of
chocolate was a mid-twentieth century American
Jewish invention."*
Sarah Jampel, "Babka's Disputed, Delicious
Origin Story," Food 52, January 18, 2022,
HTTPS://FOOD52.COM/BLOG/18792-THE-BABKA-
YOU-VE-SEEN-EVERYWHERE-ISN-T-REALLY-
BABKA-AFTER-ALL

Matriarchal fertility cake named for grandmothers,
it's more than an excuse for sixteenth-century
panettone. It's the heaven we only colloquially ·
have faith in, thanks to Poland's Queen Sforza
and Ukrainian Jews, the peasantry of pleated
skirts that its creased, tucked sides smack of.

I built it with my own progenitors, the dough
first sometimes frozen overnight for uniform
rolling, lined up like winter puddles. They never
used expensive ingredients, only bouquets of jellies,
sometimes the chewy ghosts of the fruit of the vine
they blessed, fingers covering pupils like lenses,

along with the candles that they waved hands over
three times inwards to signify the gathering of flesh,
mind, and soul. The same for rugelach and Euclidean
hamentashen—marked with their Ashkenazi prints.
With the extracting palm of hand and judicious squint
of eye is how they calculated, a language of signs

and signals interpreted by heat, translated by hours.
The question is how did exotic chocolate become

the default filling and cinnamon the streusel topping
when the ancestral Italian version contained candied
orange, citron, and lemon zest? Historians judge it
as Sephardic influence at play, but it's plain old

luxury politics: Why use just sweet when rich will
do? For my predecessors, no such verve or zing. Only
the investment for the week's end, gestures for energy
to return from where it dwelled in the scrubbing of floors,
feeding of children, endless brewing of coffee to go along
with the smokes their spouses quit too eleventh-hour to live on.

I regret eating freedom for breakfast

because it only made me hungrier
for lunch and by dinnertime I had no more

left to serve. The children had to go
without so I sent them to their beds,

telling them they should be grateful
they still had the inarguable rule of sleep.

But they just showed me the snarls
they usually keep in their thoughts.

Despite the circadian restriction
of darkness, I heard them kicking

the cardboard headboards of would-be
dreams, casting rashes of spells against

the bunting that held them close, ticking
off the ingredients to sovereignty

they would begin to gather the next day
in the first of many attempts to outgrow me.

Soccer Mom Weather

This is the full silver coin of the sun, blaring like an air horn.
This is the heat that bleaches every thread.
This is the humidity: sour, teenage feet.
This is the scuttle of cloud cover, geometries of insouciance and
    innocence.
This is the lightening siren, shrill harbinger for human resources.
This is the prismatic wind that nets coconuts, kicks off the palm
    fronds.
This is the downpour, drenching your faith in the day.
This is the puddle that soaks the stamens of your shoes, the
    unsightly blossom of the umbrella turned inside out.
This is the mud in the marsh of your car. You cool like cookies,
    hardening every second.
This is the shivering of the whistle, the end of rain delay.
These are the greening rays of the waning afternoon, steaming
    wrinkles from the field.
This is the play
          after play
            after play,
cutting loose the wild from the cultivated,
reminding you of all you once had to lose.

Considering Chagrin

> *"The Chagrin River is one of five major Lake Erie tributaries stocked by the Ohio DNR with Little Manistee strain steelhead and is a fly fisherman's delight."* —DIY Fly Fishing

My father can no longer fly fish,
can't torque the cast and its potent

energy load against his spine, narrowed
like a reed-choked river, banks growing

into the water. Nor can he wade into
a current, pit his balance against it—

not to win but to stalemate—as he flicks
the filament forward while astride

the layers of Cleveland Shale. My sister
wants to take him fishing anyway

when he visits her in Akron, re-create
the days when he used to drive her

and my brother to Lake Michigan's
parent streams for brown trout

and steelhead that steam into the sky
with no apparent trajectory, sneaking

them Labatts. Now one birthday older
than my brother will ever be, my sister

wonders if the jolting of a boat on Lake
Erie will strain the knee that lacks

cartilage, the hip that sinks like hope
ten degrees lower than the other.

The men in our family die young,
in their fifties, unpredictable

attacks grabbing them like lures
in the lip, though my father has had

a reel-screaming fight that keeps
extending the line. My brother

wanted to retire early, run a fishing
boat. In the end, my sister finds

a captain willing to go out at sunset
for two hours, who assures her

it won't be too rocky, not hot, and enough
time for my father to catch his limit.

The Foundation of the Number Six
(Is Family and a Harmonious Home)

—For Jill Lane

The day after a friend died at 51, I found
15 bees next to the laundry room, each one
a comma marking the mortal clauses of sentences,
lightened husks scratching with every turn
of the ceiling fan's staticky messages on the tile
the aging dogs have stained with their need.

I didn't know how they had gotten in, why the need
to expire en masse next to the carpet that we'd found
backpacking in Morocco, where we'd slept on tile.
Near the French doors, I noticed a lone one,
not dead but dying, wings still trying to turn,
and another in the orchid window, their sentences

easy enough to scan, bodies like tulip bulbs sentenced
to wintering. My friend hadn't received what she needed,
leaving before the season had a chance to air and turn,
short of the time the doctors guessed after they found
the tumors deep in that number-shaped gland, one
of the organs nobody can live without. The center Jenga tile.

Bees can invade a wall the same way, build tiles
until the space is owned wholly, unseen, by comb. Sentence
a hive to death or attempt a rescue—choose the one
in this case to be most effective for the host's needs,
but it will become a collage regardless, a found
poem of encaustic, zipped-up parts. Please turn

up the sounds of the universe, override whose turn
it isn't: the rich man who reads answers from digital tiles,
whose exact same stage 4 diagnosis is accurately finding
the question: *What is remission?* This whole sentence—
Nine percent—is a more tense construction. That's the need-
to-know she never told most of her friends, just the one

or two who understood such minority odds weren't the ones
ever going to be in her favor for survival. Now we slow-turn
the shiva trays, pass the pastrami, ask her children who needs
the spicy brown mustard to spread on rye stacked like tiles.
It lay in wait for her, this pre-wrapped delicatessen sentence.
In the smoke of our ancestors' genes is how we will all be found,

though sorrows of this nature seem far too deep to probe. One
apiarist finally finds the hive. He guesstimates it's six pounds, turns
his ear to the tiles, listens to the bees chew and chew these
    sentences.

Bodies of Evidence

Water has the same density as a body,
which explains the slowdown swoosh
of the mangoes once they hit the pool

like children bombing the deep end,
sending up cloud-streams of bubbles until
they drift to the grainy bottom to rest

with the other detritus. A body
in the pool either dodges the malice
of these trees, releasing like mothers

the responsibilities that hang on too long,
or takes the hits, displaying a pandemonium
of parrot feathers on the arms and shoulders

that could never be achieved by sun alone.
All summer the trees spit globules of fruit
bodies into the water, where they glow

with an alien halo for a reason nobody
can define, or torpedo what's left of
the grass, these planets a body can barely

carry the weight of for an entire
spectrum of creatures, only some of which
a body can see. They pummel the clutter

of cactus the painter and his wife replanted
under the Carrie so they wouldn't step
on spines when retouching window frames.

It's as if the land itself is both mind and body,
as if it knows why the replacing of the wood
frame of the deck, the updating of the granite

counters in the kitchen, the knocking
down of walls that don't bear anything
in order to make an open floor plan.

Where it used to embrace, now it punishes,
all the tools of the earth's body at its disposal,
the avocados speeding at car windshields

like misogynists with singular purpose
before their fall harvest, the sapodillas
and sea grapes a consistent smear of glue

in the face, the guavas assaulting
with their ripe citrine urine, the coconut
palm fronds unpredictable guillotine blades

and acorns from the live oaks a mass
explosion of shrapnel even the squirrels
reject. Every bit of destruction is a chalk mark

of guilt on the bodies who plan to sell
what really wasn't theirs to begin with,
who have only been caretaking, and who

can't guarantee that the next bodies
in line won't bring it, in pieces too terrible
to document, to the spiky, limestone ground.

There's Banishment from Native Eyes
in Sight of Native Air

*Title and quoted lines from Emily Dickinson's "I
measure every Grief I meet (561)"*

I looked away from my father's bowed head,
the same pale flesh as the oysters he ate
in Le Trappiste that he said tasted metallic,
a little too salty, though he drank their liquor
regardless, swallowing down hard on the tears
they loosed, quivering, in their last live moments.

I looked away from my mother who was looking away
from the bread basket filled with the crusty
hard ends she has always preferred to the fluff
of middles, food she can no longer digest
as she told me a story about Dover Castle
and its tunnels, where the medics practiced

their craft despite the bombs vibrating
the battlements like mallets on a tuning fork.
She recalled every detail but the one of me,
strolling beside her in the iodine dark, listening
to the audio re-enactment, panicked parables
of a war fought underground. I looked away

from the mud stains, patches like age spots,
marking our pants from the navigation of time-
bitten steps that led down to the Great River Stour
in Sandwich, where the water lay too low to search
for seals. Instead, we had headed upstream under
the old toll bridge, past centenarian Dutch barges

turned into houseboats with names like Dragonfly
and Orca, and hunchbacked banks of reeds,
bent under the weight of their own success,
where so few remain to weave them into shelter,
and I looked away from my own desire for isolation
and the image of myself crashing into the marshes,

disappearing almost instantaneously, out of range
of knees that do not bend and canes that hit
other tourists accidentally in the shins and a memory
that no longer is a busy trade hub but instead
a Cinque Port, socked in, a repository for visitors
who receive the same answers to questions

they have not asked. *Such a lapse could [not] give
them any balm.* I looked away from my second pour
of Sauvignon Blanc, my still-full pot of mussels
steamed with garlic, white wine and cream. A few
of them were closed as tight as disapproving lips,
dead already when the chef set them to flame.

Death is but one and comes but once,
Emily wrote, but my brothers visited
over and over the week we had taken to tour
Kent before I attended a conference, and there was
grief of want but there was also a want of grief,
an *imitation of a light that has so little oil*

in the vastness of the vow he had taken two years before
to no longer speak to me. I looked away from this
bitter harvest that I was tithed and thought about
the gooseberries and donut-shaped peaches, a more
succulent bounty consumed from Canterbury's
market stalls as we trekked over uneven cobblestones

to the cathedral and the tomb of the Black Prince,
where candles burned for those cherished and lost,
and for those who have failed to appear. My brother
had married a Catholic woman and baptized his children
but in a moment of premonition requested a Jewish
funeral. In two months from then, it would be Yom Kippur,

the day we repent our sins and mourn our dead, whether recent
or long past, and we would spark the yahrzeit candle for him
to melt into its glass all night and day. I have many deceits
from which I cannot look away but not this: When my father
lifted his head from his empty plate and said, "What's done
is done," I assured him that I had already chosen to forgive.

III.

"The voices all ran together
so that I tasted them in the taste of the mango,
a sharp gravel in the flesh."

—Mary Oliver

The Sound of Zero Copula

The end doesn't come with rattlesnake breath.
Sometimes it sneaks in with silence as its voice.
Haven't we known that the song is a myth,

that swans protect life with mostly a hiss?
The tunes we expel are never our choice.
The end doesn't come with rattlesnake breath.

The rest between beats is its own small death,
a pause for the pump to prime its hot sauce.
Haven't we known that the song is a myth?

The brash illnesses that muzzle us brief
others on how to indulge in this vice.
The end doesn't come with rattlesnake breath,

the blare of early warning systems. Thief
of all sound who cuts alarms to the house.
Haven't we known that the song is a myth?

No flutes. No horns. No soundtrack to bequeath.
And this, too: we admit ourselves wordless.
The end doesn't come with rattlesnake breath.
Haven't we known that the song is a myth?

Antonomasia

After Concert in the Egg *by Hieronymus Bosch*

Never mind the snake
hanging like a stale piece

of licorice over a pinky of branch;
he's not so seductive after all.

And though trees root here, and myths
teem like gods, this pessimistic

impasto is hardly a garden.
Never mind the choir of goliards

chanting from a common score
inside the cracked amphitheater

of an egg. They wear the foundations
of birds and buildings on their heads

as if brains are fertilized yolks,
sprouting the concrete. Never mind

the roasted chicken aloft
in the wicker, the grilled fish,

the hand reaching for it, the other
hand cutting away from the monk

the string attached to his tithed purse.
Never mind the cat contemplating

all this delicious theft. Some
appetites are better left unexplored.

Still, music can turn men into animals
and back again, it seems: The lute player

wears the head of a donkey
with no apparent discomfort

as he plucks and strums. A monkey
chews on a horn. Can he evolve?

Upright, inside the egg, a yokel
fingers a harp, another a penny whistle.

The conductor spears a baton
like a lightning rod, a spire

on a cathedral, a direct line
to strike-you-down morality.

Never mind him; no one else is.
Nor is anyone paying attention

to the tiny men of conscience
in the corner, busily working

overtime, forging nightmares.
And never mind the turtle.

No, really, never mind the turtle
as he makes his tortured way

across the panel. He is a lowly
whole note that has escaped

the sheet music, the staffs that prove
the artist died before these

lead-tin-yellows and madder lakes
tipped the hand-glued sable

of any brush. Never mind,
never mind. Take this alchemy

into your mouth like a vitamin
and hum it. On the palate,

the building blocks of creation
crumble into acrid aftertaste.

My Hairstylist Is a Man Who Loves the Shape of a Woman's

skull, its petite cliffs and canyons that he hikes
with his agile fingers, the dips and curves in
the road of a scalp that he reads like a triptych.
Otherwise indifferent, his Gucci model face
set as if for a permanent advertisement,

he converses only with the Italian men whose hair
he trims in between foiling and painting away
my personality, turning me as platinum and beach-
wave as every other woman in Miami. He envisions
me even less visibly than I view myself, I think,

until we go to the sink, and I lean back in the chair
while he rocks and cradles my head in his palms
the size of saucers, supporting my occipital
bone like a lizard caught to take outside, turning
me this way and that under the faucet, exploring

the only part of my aging body that interests him,
my drenched and gleaming skull showing off
its faulty crevices and divots like a landscape
or perhaps an archeological excavation, ancient
and revelatory, perpetually in danger of collapse.

At Riverbend Park

After At Riverbend Park *by Ralph Papa*

Improbable birds, why have they settled
on the banks of the Loxahatchee to become

sawgrass and cattail for the day? Thatched,
swampy roof, their wings are neither question

nor answer but a landscape of both, partners
to the current dredged by the peacock's careless tail.

This is no serenity spell. Under them, the blood
from Seminoles continues to run, the soil so much

more magenta than the feathers of the roseate spoonbill.
The sandhill crane is a barren citrus tree; the flocks

of parrots behead the palms when they lift away,
leaving only the echoes of their complaints behind.

Trophic Cascade

On introducing wolves back into Yellowstone
National Park in 1995

We feared the mastication of cartilage
would be perceptible in every part of the park,
translate to swing-setted backyards.

But we were not ever the prey.
We were always the teeth that took
the shoots from the valleys,

crippling cottonwoods, keeping
beavers from building dams
with ripe, fallen aspens.

Without us, the rivers in gorges
are smiles with pools like dimples,
fixing their banks in time.

Promise City by the Numbers

Within driving distance
of unincorporated Confidence,

located in the middle
of the bottom of the state,

this Midwest town has a population
a mere fraction of its cemetery:

112 according to the last
census, divided into 49

households and 29 families,
all but 0.9 of whom are the color

of the space between stanzas.
Not much happens in Promise.

Most work. Poverty is work, too.
So is marriage. Birth and death

are the same as everywhere else,
no more remarkable, no less

to grieve. Main Street runs
mundane through it all, offering

Main Street kinds of items:
signposts, supplements, floss

for your teeth. But today,
a church day, the wind is a sip

of sparkling lemonade from the west
at 9 miles per hour, the air a balmy

69 degrees and the humidity is more
like Miami at 99 percent. It's clear

that spring has come on gopher feet
to the prairie, bringing the time

to restore the blended colors
of the mesic turf with the seeds

of black-eyed Susan and smooth
blue aster. Invest in it. Revel.

For the next 90 days, attract
pollinators with blazing star

and showy goldenrod, bring back
independent bison to graze

like mailmen through all kinds
of weather, who will later tunnel

through 9 months of cemented snow
with the determined shovels

of their hooves to find ox-eye,
goat's rue, and rattlesnake master,

who lead themselves to water
at deceptive local ponds

that don't freeze all the way down
to their muddy seats, and give

eco-tours to curious tourists
driving cross-country, allowing

the wealthy to hunt the herds
and feast on meat tasting

of sovereign natures and a place
living wildly up to its name.

A Contrapuntal of Light-Dependent Reactions

the surface shoots of spring
>photosynthesize into warrens

adored by ants and mining bees
>o protector of pollen and seed of
>>bloodroots

see how the *sanguinaria* burrows through
>these blossoms in bare relief

leaves clasping petals
>like chapped hands in prayer

communal rovers they are
>never quite released

Searching for the Florida Panther,
I Find Only Signs

Catamount. Cougar. Mountain lion
of the prairie, subspecies of the puma.
Prowler, predator, killer of dormant
cattle chewing on hay reaped from
the rough soil fertilized by ancient

oysters. Taker of tiny dogs who have
wandered too far from ranch houses
stretched on limestone foundations,
who have always traveled in the seats
of a manufactured way of life. I lay

all the names I've been told to fear
on my tongue like paint, thick and dry
as if improperly stored, the animal
I long to hold up at the other end of
a cell phone camera or capture safely

in the rearview mirror of my car. Raw
umber ghosts of the hammocks coming
back to growth after a fire, they offer
no gifts aside from scat and shadow.
Rumor and innuendo. And this framing

of their forms *en plein air,* stamped as if
in charcoal on cautionary metal, staked
every few miles on the shoulder of
a highway gripping the River of Grass
with the invisible tentacles of canvas.

Kings and Queens

A true conch musician brings their own shell.
Battle trumpet, shofar shaped by sea swells,
instrument of high praise and forfeiture—
doesn't it make sense to hone your lips' purse
to all that's so grand and ceremonial

on something uniquely royal? There will
be discoveries like in the Marsoulas
from 17,000 years before—
a true conch

that was probably shared, ancestral,
passed down through generations of temple
players. But even orchestral, we wear
an idiosyncratic embouchure
for a true conch.

Face Value

Just when I think there is nothing left to be exhumed

—an entire body of introverted odors forced into sunlight,
                    handcuffed to bags

of activated charcoal, the fossilized lace of termite wings
                    glinting in piles,

every last jar of mango salsa, pried open to carousel
                    the disposal—

the house coughs up a homemade bank, Hills Bros coffee can
                    of electric perk covered

with a tri-colored clown suit and cap that my great-aunt Ida had
    knit.
                    The white parts yellowed.

The yellows—more of time's jaundice. The eyes still pasted on, one
                    higher than the other.

Inside, uncirculated coins my grandmother had divided, straight
    from the teller,
                    every Hanukkah and Passover

—three for me, three for my sister, four for my brother (more for
    him,
                    the oldest and a boy).

We called them silver dollars. They weren't bullion but
    commemorative

                Eisenhower dollars

with bald eagles and Liberty Bells on the obverse (followed by JFK
    and Susan B. Anthony

after that president went out of style), substantial and serious,
    always chilled

                like my father's post-rush

hour coat. We did nothing but save them, playing dreidel instead
    with the gold

                -wrapped chocolate

coins that smelted, igneous tin, when you held them too long. A
    third kind of gelt

                my grandmother tended

we weren't allowed to touch. These were the seedpods of the
    honesty plant,

                the papery moon-parings

veined like taro root chips. The French call them "the Pope's
    money;" the Dutch,

                "coins of Judas."

My Polish grandmother grew them on her side of the duplex
    apartment's stoop,

                dried them to display

under the spider plants and their dangling, intergenerational pups.
    For luck

                or for beauty,

I can't recall, I longed to pluck and palm those incandescent, forbidden

shavings of silver,

more valuable to me than politicians and candy. I never dared disobey.

Nor did I open

what was one last childhood gift for me alone—a whole roll of Bicentennial

quarters. Today,

like the seeds of honesty, they're uncorrupted in their wrapper, sturdy as a pledge,

labeled with the singular

remains of my grandmother's hand. I take a picture and send it to my father,

who emails back,

You're rich. He's kidding. It's ten dollars. Still, I hold the hard currency

of a different age,

her pointed script, tight in my fist. A bare fit. This is enough wealth to grip.

I Pose

For a Selfie with Venom

My Termite Service Technician

Who Is Still Sometimes Recognized

as His Nineties UFC Persona,

as a fist
as a fist the inconsistent growth silhouette
as a fist the inconsistent growth silhouette of an heirloom tomato
as a fist the inconsistent growth silhouette of an heirloom tomato
    furrowed by the paths of insects

as an insect
as an insect that burrows
as an insect that burrows in the humid flesh and juice
as an insect that burrows in the humid flesh and juice of tropical
    wood frame houses

as a house
as a house like a retired competitor
as a house like a retired competitor on his second career
as a house like a retired competitor again invested in the
    opposition

as the opposition
as the opposition who drinks
as the opposition who drinks holistic remedies as if to purge
as the opposition who drinks holistic remedies as if to purge the
    losses of fights and women

as a woman
as a woman also giving
as a woman also giving up
as a woman also giving up what she has won and loves and loathes

Self Help Q-and-A at Zoo da Maia*

What are you struggling against that you can simply release?

> The brown bear paces, relentless as a telemarketer. Each
> time he hits the wall he turns, an Olympic swimmer
> pushing away in a twist, then dangles one paw over the
> artificial cliff that drops down to water where there is no
> egg-stuffed salmon for him to snatch from the current,
> where there is no current, where the pool is stagnant as
> tenure. He creates his own draft until his hip bones stand
> akimbo in his tailwinded coat. This could be taken as
> persistence, if I wish—

What deep needs do you have that aren't getting met?

> The family of monkeys, jealous of the sea lion applauding
> with flippers on cue for sardines, makes like Wallendas until
> the keeper distracts them with peeling heads of lettuce, a
> pail of apples. I know this pelting is also routine—

How are you living or behaving inauthentically?

> A sign warns that the zebras will bite, but they crowd the
> fence for handouts. They are equine dad bods but for one,
> who is pregnant; a tattoo of hoofs dents her stripes. I, too,
> feel on display, pulled taut for all to see—

How are you behaving as a reactor rather than an initiator?

> The flamingos shiver on one collective leg. The caimans and
> alligators fail to find mud. The trichotillomaniac lion picks
> at his geriatric mane. Also a dweller of tropics, a resident in

turns of savannas and rainforests, I too have no other layer
of dander, feather, leather, fur—

*How are you censoring what you really think or feel because you're
afraid?*

At the bird show, the vultures are reluctant as student
drivers to wing after carrion placed on platforms, but
eventually draw their inverse arc low over the heads of
the audience. I protect my uncovered hair, patchy from
stress and middle age. I have already seen on the quay what
unexpected offerings can plop into a wineglass—

*What are you leaving unresolved or unfinished that needs your
attention?*

The tigers crouch and pant, crouch and pant, though the
sun is toothless behind the taint of clouds. They are a
"fearful symmetry" when the species from the neighboring
exhibit, cautious and inglorious, stumbles into view,
launching themselves at the barrier that rebuffs their
charge. I trace the glass where it is cracked like desert-
taught skin, bracketing the breath of prey—

*Questions are adapted from "60 Deep Questions to Ask Yourself to Create
'Aha' Moments" by Barrie Davenport at HTTPS://LIVEBOLDANDBLOOM.COM/02/
MINDFULNESS/DEEP-QUESTIONS-ASK. "Fearful symmetry" is from William Blake's
"The Tyger."

It's about the dog, but not really about the dog,

which is why I continue to cry at odd moments
popping up in my day like advertisements on

social media several weeks after we found her
dead in her crate, a cold log of dachshund,

the other two dogs who had slept there with her
for fourteen years eager to scramble out and pee

on the fallen toast of palm fronds outside, come back in
to crunch kibble and take another nap, do all the normal

dog things that they do, as if they didn't notice anything
wrong. It's about how they knew, having curled around

her body sinking into that foreign place all night,
but also about how they really didn't know, or want

to understand, how they look up at me now every time
I walk in the door, my arms empty of her, then settle

their heads on their paws with a single, mutual sigh,
and give her plot on the cushion the girth of a large belt.

Or it's about how I project these feelings onto
them, the loss, the space, the childhoods she held

in her comedian's body of both of my kids
and the length of time that we lived in this house

that we can now clean of her final traces to put

on the market for a family with babies and different

kinds of pets, who want an acre of yard with too many
mango trees and scenery that Facebook identifies

as India instead of Miami. It's about the mangoes,
which the dachshund scavenged for only one season

and inexplicably never ate again, but also not really
about the mangoes, which I don't have energy to gather

anymore; she preferred the half-rotten avocadoes
anyway, sneaking over to the pair of trees marking

the property line by the fence every time I let
all three dogs out at night, coming back with

the mottled shell of fruit in her snout, or the sugary
sapodillas, brown as rats, rooting like a pig in the brush

as if for truffles. It's about this nest but really also not
about this nest, emptying though not vacant yet, built

by a raptor though I am now a sparrow or whatever kind
of bird a bird of prey hunts. But oh, how I recall that raptor,

how I still want to eagle the sky and look down
on the world the way I did when I felt it owed me

something enormous that I didn't have to earn or catalogue
or think about the day I would have to downsize it away.

After We Move, We Learn about the Miami Supreme: A Matriarchal Shrub

Masked and shielded in this home barely worn,
we nurse the gardenia budding by the door.

> We nurse the gardenia budding by the door.
> The neighbors, still new to us, call it iconic.

The neighbors, still new to us, call it iconic,
say it's as ancient as solitude and folklore.

> They say it's as ancient as solitude, folklore,
> its perfume enough to posy the block.

Its perfume is enough to posy the block,
alert the thieves. We nourish hope like a habit.

> Alert as thieves, we nourish hope like a habit.
> The blossoming is public though none of us are.

The blossoming is public though none of us are,
masked and shielded in this home, now so worn.

Evaporating Villanelle for *Emotion #2*

After EMOTION #2 *by Walter Brown*

Grief arrives often into the middle
of things, interjected like a comma
that survives, woven into the saddle

of a list chosen by Oxford for battle,
twanging every axon in the soma.
Grief arrives often into the middle

and rarely softens,
demagoguery
that survives, woven

into the sodden
season, sharp-eyed, spry.
Grief arrives, sudden

serrated knives.
Fabric frayed
that survives—

defended;
amended.
Grief arrives.
That survives.

I praise my neighbors

who allow their engineered Labradoodles
    and French bulldogs to urinate on the "No Pee"
        signs staked into the balding pate of my front

lawn, the citric liquid searing what's left of
    the grass day after day, who extend the leashes
        as far as the historic brick walkway, clipped

off like bangs halfway into the yard. I want to be
    as brave as they are, watching their ornamental dogs'
        legs arabesque over the cast iron silently

castigating them in front of the crepe myrtle draped
    with the ironed hippie hair of Spanish moss
        and the weeping crimson bottlebrush, knotted

by air plants, ribboned with hummingbirds. I applaud
    their camouflaged, collective gaze, as impassive to criticism
        as a referee, how it pays no attention to me sitting

less than twenty feet away in the window of the Tudor
    house that once belonged to the Capone family, where
        the attic is haunted by auburn and emerald iguanas

jetéing from the top of the overgrown live oak,
    and I hide my jewelry, what little of it is left,
        my grandmothers' opal rings stolen when I lived

on South Beach, behind the false wall that once shielded shotguns.
    This courage: It is an unearned, misplaced brilliance.
        It is an ostentation of peafowl, bobbing down the
        middle

of my suburban street, indifferent to the flocks of bicycles imploring
    them to move, matching every bell and whistle with a war cry
        of their own, as mystified, perhaps, as all of us the
        reason

they are here but certain of their right to stay. It is
    the sound I need to sample, to re-broadcast in continuous
        four-bar loops, rather than the jeweled *good-morning*
        voice,

the *I-don't-like-to-make-trouble-when-I'm-new-here* voice,
    the *I-clean-up-the-mess-of-my-own-dogs voice,* instead
        of letting polished symbols speak this message for me.

Birkat Habayit: A Woman Is a Bird When

After Empowered Women *by*
Tomas Valdivieso Valto

Wood under feet, dressed in flower parts,
she surveys her private garden, ragtag,
everything in it equal to her heart.

Downsize, they tell her. It's only a start.
Learn to bolster what's beginning to sag.
Wood under feet, dressed in flower parts,

a woman is a thorn, poisonous dart.
Planes fly away from the kite of her back,
everything in them equal to her heart;

convertibles accordion, roofs hard.
Oh, to feel again the pain of the egg.
Wood under feet, dressed in flower parts,

A woman goes rogue, winging wide, apart,
her flock caught in a current of jet lag,
everything in it equal to her heart.

One eye doll-wide, one squinting an alert,
she talons her home like a prized handbag,
wood under feet, dressed in flower parts,
everything in it equal to her heart.